SAP CRM Interview Questions, Answers, and Explanations

SAPCOOKBOOK.COM

TABLE OF CONTENTS

SAP CRM Interview Questions, Answers, and Explanations

By Scott Cameron

SAPCOOKBOOK
Equity Press

Introduction

During my career as an SAP implementer, I have been asked a wide range of SAP Questions. They range from business strategy, functional and technical questions.

Throughout this book questions and answers will be varied because SAP CRM is an amalgamation of tiers within the SAP CRM platform.

Unlike R/3, which has a distinct three tier architecture, CRM is best represented by a Venn diagram.

CRM Platform Model

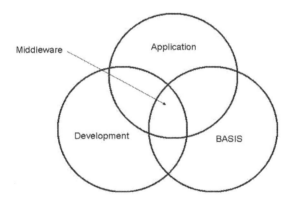

The following questions are not targeted to one specific (application) area or tier of the platform but instead are a mix of technical, functional and business questions.

Section 1 Strategic and Setup Questions

This section outlines some of the more commonly asked questions pertaining to CRM best practices as well as questions pertaining to the setup of your CRM environments.

☞ QUESTION 1

Organization Model

What is the difference between standard backend version and enhanced back end version of organization model?

✍ ANSWER

The enhanced version allows for multiple assignments of a single object. As an example, in R3, a sales group can be assigned to multiple sales offices. In the standard organization model, this is not possible.

As SAP's CRM product has evolved, it has become more compatible with the R3 product. Before CRM 4.0, it was not possible to assign an organization object to more than one organizational object. This was a problem for many SAP customers because in R/3, it is possible. So in 4.0 and after, SAP introduced the ability to handle multiple assignments and a program to convert the org model to this structure.

So if your client has R/3 organization model that involves multiple assignments, you will need the enhanced version.

☞ QUESTION 2

Creation of a Business Partner

I have several questions.

1) While creating a business partner in CRM enterprise, it asked for BP role.

I created it with a role prospect. Later on, this partner has given me some business. Shall I create a new record for this business partner or change the existing partner record like a 'prospect to sell to party'.

2) Who creates the business partners? Is it an end user or a functional consultant?

For example, if I created a prospect in CRM enterprise on production server and in due course, this business partner have given me some business. Shall I create a new BP record of role sold to party or change the existing record from BP role prospect to BP sold to party?

✍ ANSWER

It depends on specific situations and required functionalities. If you are talking about a project mode where you as a consultant are customizing and developing, for example CRM online, you might want to have a master data to test your configuration. In that case, you probably will create some of your own master data simply to test everything you are configuring (development system).

On a production system however, it is usually the end user

who creates the master data, such as business partners, products, etc.

The company however should decide if for example every sale should be able to create new prospects/customers in the system, or if this should happen via a single point of entry (1 team responsible for creating and maintaining master data).

You would have to change the classification of the business partner (see tab page classification hours) from prospect to customer.

Again, where you do it depends on your setup. Which system is leading (CRM or R/3) and who are prospects or customers replicated from one system to the other.

☞ QUESTION 3

Use of R/3 conditions in CRM

We are trying to replicate SAP R/3 pricing conditions to CRM.

Initial download of pricing customizing has been done. R/3 pricing conditions are displayed in CRM customizing well (pricing, rebates and free goods).

Though when I go in customizing (in CRM) to use these R/3 conditions in condition maintenance under "marketing planning and campaign management",

I can see my rebates conditions, the free goods conditions but not the other conditions applying directly in the sales order.

I have checked the configuration for the conditions not shown. They are categorized in:

Application = CRM;
Usage 'PR' for pricing;
Source R/3;

Is there any particular reason for this?

✍ ANSWER

Conditions created in R/3 and replicated to CRM can only be maintained in R/3. If your middleware is set properly, any changes (VK11, VK12) will replicate to CRM.

Only conditions created in CRM are maintained in CRM (most likely documents that do not replicate back to R/3, if that scenario exists for you).

If you are trying to create condition records for a marketing campaign, you will need to do a couple of things:

1. Maintain the "condition maintenance group" to include the condition type and table for maintenance context CAMPAIGN;

2. In R/3, designate that this condition type is maintained in CRM;

☞ **QUESTION 4**

SAP NetWeaver

I have a couple of questions about the SAP Netweaver:

1] Is it necessary to work in SAP Netweaver environment to configure/customize SAP CRM modules especially IC Webclient and Internet Sales even though the company does not have SAP BW/SAP APO in its System Landscape Design?

2] If so, then as SAP CRM consultant, what are the necessary things to know about SAP Netweaver?

✍ **ANSWER**

The answers are provided according to the number they were asked:

1. You are indeed working in SAP Netweaver environment. SAP Netweaver is an open platform for integration purposes. In fact, for you as a consultant, you will probably not have much to do with SAP Netweaver, unless you would be doing XI or BW.

   You can use CRM as a standalone application or integrated with SAP R/3 and/or BW. Depending on what the customer will be implementing, you will of course have a different system landscape.

2. Just do some reading on SAP Netweaver technology. You don't need to get into real detail. Just check out information on help.sap.com or on service.sap.com. There is a lot of information available.

☞ QUESTION 5

Enterprise Portal

What exactly is Enterprise Portal and in what way do SAP CRM Consultants connect to it?

What are the activities that they have to do in EP?

✍ ANSWER

The enterprise portal is a Portal which allows people to have a single point of access to different applications, tools, and other information sources.

For example, it is possible to have via single sign on the SAP EP (enterprise portal) access to CRM processes like marketing and campaign management, service processes , but at the same time access to BW reports and or queries, and database access to non SAP database related data.

Integration in the SAP portal for CRM is via I-Views. It is called People Centric CRM and the screens that you integrate in the portal are PCUI screens. Another thing is BSP developments (BSP applications like the IC Webclient – via Transaction code SE80 you can look up the BSP application CRM_IC, which is the IC Webclient BSP Application for the IC Webclient) that can be integrated in the SAP Portal.

SAP delivers those working assets in the form of Portal Roles, like for example CALL Center Agent, or Marketing Manager. Every role gives access to specific work sets which give access to specific Iviews or screens.

☞ **QUESTION 6**

Deploying SAP CRM Projects

What is the implementation tool/methodology that is generally used in deploying SAP CRM projects? Is it ASAP or Solution Manager?

✍ **ANSWER**

You can use the SAP Solution Manager as a customer platform for efficient implementation and operation of SAP Solutions such as the mySAP Business Suite (CRM). It makes use of the mentioned ASAP (key accelerated SAP implementation concepts).

The way I approach things is usually the following (supposing that the customer is considering implementing SAP CRM):

1) First you analyze business requirements. What processes are being used? Are the processes working in an optimal way?

2) What processes need to be improved? How can you improve them from a business perspective?

3) Make AS-IS analysis of the current business process and designs the TO BE processes.

4) Translate the TO BE processes into system processes such as marketing and campaign management, account and contact management, IC win or Webclient, complaint or case management.....

5) Consider complexity, cost, added value, ease of use, user acceptation, implementation time and budget, during the BLUEPRINT phase.

6) During the BLUEPRINT phase, it is likely that you do not know what SAP functionalities within CRM are existing, and are best to implement. Therefore I usually do a lot of research on different sources.

I usually read SAP HELP, search presentations, Online knowledge products and other information on help.sap. com or on service.sap.com (make sure you get a S-user and password on this site) look at SAP notes and also ask questions on forums like sapfans.com or others. But one of the best search tools for SAP functionality are internet search engines, such as Google.

☞ **QUESTION 7**

The Most important and Mandatory Functions

Which are the most important and mandatory functions, function modules and Transaction codes of IC Webclient, Marketing and Base Customization?

✍ **ANSWER**

I suggest you follow existing courses like the:

- CR100: CRM base customizing
- CR600: Marketing and Campaign management
- CR400: IC Winclient
- CR410: IC Webclient

If you have access to a CRM system, you will discover the Transaction codes easily!

In the SAP Menu, you can click open the relevant folders, and display the Transaction codes by displaying the technical names.

To do so, in the menu: you do "Extras> Settings> Display technical names".

For Customizing you can check also the relevant paths: Customizing is done via Transaction code SPRO.

Look up function modules via transaction code SE37. Business Add-ins via SE18. (Usually relevant BAdI's are also mentioned in customizing under the relevant path).

In order to understand how everything works, I advise you first to read existing documentation (power points about for example IC Webclient, SAP help information) and also the relevant Customizing documentation.

☞ QUESTION 8

General System landscape for CRM Projects

What is the system landscape design for CRM projects? What are the integration points within CRM and with other systems?

✍ ANSWER

The system landscape for CRM or any SAP Module usually looks like this:

A) Development system (here you do all customizing settings and developments).

B) QA (quality assurance system): for end user training and especially for unit testing and integration testing purposes.

C) Productive system.

SAP CRM is for example usually integrated with a backbone SAP R/3 system. Integration in this case happened via the CRM middleware. On both sides (R/3 = plug in and CRM you will have a R/3 adapter).

For integration with BW there exists a BW Adapter. (In the CRM system, SAP delivers by the way standard data sources that can be used by the BW system. They can be activated (content) and replicated to the BW System for data analysis.

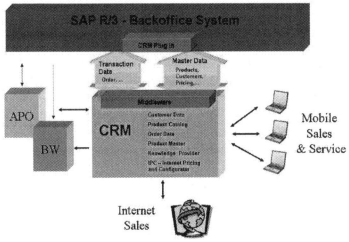

☞ QUESTION 9

Webclient vs Winclient

I am new to CRM & wanted to go for Interaction Center training. Before doing so, however, I'd like to know a few things:

What is the difference between Interaction Center Winclient & Interaction Webclient?

Do I need to attend both trainings?

✎ ANSWER

The User Interface, that's the difference for Winclient dynpro and for Webclient BSP. Since most likely you're familiar with dynpro's and the business logic is the same for both UIs I'd recommend for you to attend the Webclient training.

Winclient is using the typical SAPGUI whereas the Webclient is based on BSP developments (standard BSP applications CRM_IC or CRM_IC_AUTO for automotive industry).

The courses available are:

    CR400: IC Winclient
    CR410: IC Webclient

I followed both courses, and depending on what you want to implement or what the customer will be implementing you should best follow the specific course!

You should know that the basic principles (processes and

functionalities) are the same within both user interfaces. SAP however still supports IC Winclient, but new developments are focused on the IC Webclient.

In case of performance and stability you are better of with the Winclient, although SAP is running up on that matter also for the Webclient. SAP claims that both UI should be comparable!

Furthermore, from an end user perspective, the way of using the two tools, is quite different. The Webclient is much more user friendly and the overview is much easier and intuitive.

Customizing for both applications is done separately.

You will have a separate customizing path for IC Winclient and for IC Webclient. (They overlap however sometimes, so do not implement both UI at the same time on the same server).

The IC Webclient is much more flexible, since you can 'easily' change screen fields, screens, layout and stuff like that! But I would not take easy in a literal way. You can integrate your own BSP developments in the IC Webclient, and also R/3 processes and or Internet pages.

To implement the Webclient, I advise everyone to take a look at the IC Webclient Cookbook (available on Service. sap.com), check the available PowerPoint's on this matter; read the SAPHelp (IC Webclient and Winclient), and follow the training!

Typically you will need following resources:

- Functional consultant who understands call center processes can analyze customer requirements; customize

the IC Win or Webclient;
- ABAP Programmer (object oriented programming knowledge is required -methods, BADI's;
- BSP developer (MVC -model view controller concepts knowledge, html and xml knowledge);

Some additional information:

SAPHelp Information is available on:

http://help.sap.com/saphelp_crm40sr1/helpdata/en/b3/bb c13806684a1eb86b2821ab92827f/frameset.htm

Online Knowledge products are available on (special S-UserID and password required however, and also access to the necessary information:

[url]service.sap.com/okp[/url]

Should you have access, the path would be:

SAP Consultant Education > Early product training>SAP Online Knowledge products>SAP Online knowledge products>SAP CRM 4.0

Or know they have posted 5.0 documentation

☞ QUESTION 10

Interview Questions faced with IC Webclient, et. al.

When interviewing a possible candidate, what are the interview questions that I should ask in relevance to IC Webclient, Marketing, and Base Customization?

✍ ANSWER

Here are some probabilities:

- Project experience?
- CRM functional knowledge? Which components?
- Technical knowledge (abap, oss notes implementations, BSP and html knowledge)?
- What are best practice cases? What is the added value?
- Show functional experience (e.g. how to create marketing plan, campaign, target groups, and sent out email to existing target group....) and customizing knowledge... (know what is possible, but also the limitations)
- Why IC Webclient instead of IC Winclient?
- What about performance of IC Webclient?
- What about User interface differences and customer adaptation and training?
- Possibility to show a small demo (stay in SAP Standard delivery) in short notice?

☞ QUESTION 11

Whether to replicate R/3 sales order to CRM

I need some advice. I am implementing CRM for a new client and they used quite a few sales order types and wanted to bring these entire Sales Order over to CRM.

What are the key factors to consider in replicating the existing R/3 sales orders to CRM? What do we lose if we do not replicate these Sales Order's over?

If I want to see the past sales order history with the customers within CRM guys (not from the web), do I need to replicate the sales order over? Are there other means of seeing these orders?

Is it common to replicate other sales order types such as KA, KB, KE KR, RE, CR and DR? I can understand why CR and DR are required but am not sure about the others.

✍ ANSWER

I guess it could depend on your interaction channel. As an example, if you want to show the order status in the ISA web shop, you will need to have the documents replicated to CRM.

It is likely that in your business partner fact sheet, you will want to include an info block that displays sales order history and allows for drill down into the transactions. Open Orders and Orders for the last n months, that kind of thing. If so, I would bring these documents over to CRM.

Your succeeding question's answers depend on who your CRM users will be and what data they need.

☞ QUESTION 12

How can I get Sales Order from R/3 to CRM

I want to know how to transfer the sales order from R/3 to CRM, and how to bill for that particular Sales Order such that it replicates in R/3.

My Scenario is:

I have to get the Sales Order from R/3 and I have to bill for that particular Sales Order in CRM and this bill document has to replicate R/3 also.

✍ ANSWER

Billing does not replicate from CRM to R/3, but the financial data will transfer to R/3 F/I (just no invoice in VF02, VF03).

To transfer the order it has to be configured in both systems and middleware parameters set up.

☞ QUESTION 13

What ID to use to login to XCM Configuration for user administration

I am currently following the BP CRM Internet Sales (C14) guide to configure the internet sales settings.

There is a step (4.1.41) asking me to log on to http://<host>:port/isauseradmin/admin/xcm/init.do to enter the configuration parameters.

However, I encountered: 'The requested resource does not exist' error. I have checked with the Basis person and he has no idea why the system does not recognize the URL. I have tried using a different URL such as http://<host>:port/B2B/admin/xcm/init.do and was prompted for ID and password, but ironically we do not know what ID and password to use.

Why is this happening?

✍ ANSWER

The ISA application is installed on the Java Server (if your basis person did that). So when you click the link and it asks you for the login and password, it refers to the Java Server on which the ISA resides.

☞ QUESTION 14

Initial Download for CUSTOMER_MAIN

I have some problems I would like some help with:

Problem 1:

I started initial download from R/3 system for object CUSTOMER_MAIN. I set the filter criteria in CUSTOMER_ MAIN for downloading 10 customers from the table KNA1. This is just to cross check whether the download is happening correctly or not.

Now in monitor (transaction: R3AM1), the status of object CUSTOMER_MAIN is shown running a long time. I checked all queues, and no data is stuck. In R/3, outbound queue, R3AD_CUSTOM* indicated 'status STOP'. It stops the delta queue during the initial download.

There is one strange thing that I observed, my 10 BP are downloaded to table CRMM_BUT_CUSTNO, and however, table BUT000 is empty. Shouldn't It be downloaded to table BUT000 doesn't it?

I also went to TR SMQ1 (outbound queue) in R/3, double clicked on STOP for queue R3AD_CUSTOME*, it gives the informative pop up "Set by Host name: CARDEVDP; Transaction: Report: SAPMSSY1". I also checked the RFC connection, and it is fine.

I found one dump in CRM in transaction ST22 saying "call function not found". Upon double clicking, it says the following:

"The function module "BUPA_DEF_ADDRESS_ DELTA_QUEUE_A" was called, but cannot be found in the Function Library: Error in the ABAP application program. The current ABAP program "CL_IM_BP_BW_ UPD===============CP" had to be terminated because one of the statements could not be executed."

This is probably due to an error in the ABAP program.

I searched the SAP note for this, but did not get anything remotely close to the problem.

Problem 2:

PI_BASIS was upgraded to the highest level at both CRM and R/3. So now CUSOTMER_MAIN is GREEN (status DONE) in monitor. Still, the table BUT000 is empty. I checked all queues in R/3 and CRM, and no data is stuck. I went to SMW01 and in there are many entries having each block size of 100 and by double clicking, I can see the BP, but the status of BDOC's description here is "Received (intermediate state)" with YELLOW light.

In ST22, it shows the same status as above. Also, BUPA_ DEF_ADDRESS_DELTA_QUEUE_A function module is not available in CRM and in R/3. But this is shown available in BW. I don't understand what is happening. What could be wrong here and how do I fix the problem?

✍ ANSWER

Answers are provided according to the numbers they were asked:

1. Check the function module "BUPA_DEF_ADDRESS_

DELTA_QUEUE_A" if it is active. This might be where the problem lies.

2. Depending on the version of the CRM you are using, check to see in transaction SMW01 for the object 'CUSTOMER_ MAIN'.

☞ **QUESTION 15**

EEWB is not very flexible

We only want to see the Customer Data Tab for 'Person'. Not for Organization or Group.

The BP transaction has been extended with a New Table and CI using the EEWB (Easy Enhancement Work Bench).

Does anyone know how I might display the Customer Data conditionally only for a certain BUT000-TYPE. (VALUES: 1 = Person, 2 = Organization, 3 = Group)?

✍ **ANSWER**

You can use TRANSACTION CODE: BUPT. Create a new Data Set and assign the View that got created via EEWB. Now add this Data Set to your desired BP role. This way, your new file will be only visible to that particular role, and not on any other screens.

Just remember when using the EEWB that if you replicate your objects it will revert all other object back to standard. Thus you will and can lose other objects created within the EEWB. So as a final setup you should copy or replicate your programs into the other standard SAP development tools, such as a standard BADI as an example.

☞ QUESTION 16

Business Partner replication

My client has had an R/3 system already up and running for two years and now the legacy CRM system has to be replaced by SAP CRM. The thing is that customer numbers in R/3 are assigned manually by the users while using a certain self made up logic. The client's wish is to keep on having R/3 leading with assigning customer numbers manually.

In the old legacy system, customer numbers that are not replicated to R/3 were assigned by the system. I now have to find a way to convert the legacy CRM system to SAP CRM.

What if a customer, for example, has BP number 100 in CRM and customer number 200 in the R/3 system?

If the R/3 number is added to the BP in CRM as an external number, would it be possible to have data replication from CRM to R/3 purely based on the external number and not the CRM BP number?

If so, how is this realized?

Is it possible to have a business partner replication between CRM (4.0) and R/3 purely based on the external partner number which is the partner number in R/3?

If so, how is this accomplished?

Can this be customized or does this require additional programming?

✍ ANSWER

Apply a filter to the middleware object to control which customers are distributed from R/3 to CRM? Or are you asking if you can accept the number from R/3 as an external number to CRM when the BP is created in CRM?

In any case, the answer to both is yes.

You will also need to decide which system is to be the point of origin for these customers and then do an initial load in order to create the customers on the other system. After that you can decide where and how on-going maintenance will be done.

If you are trying to link up existing customers between R/3 and CRM, check configuration guide (replication). There's a chapter dedicated to number ranges strategies. In that chapter, there's also a strategy discussed where business partners in CRM and R/3 have different number ranges.

☞ **QUESTION 17**

How to deal with different destination in CRM

I need some advice as to the best way I can go about bringing the customer's master data over to CRM.

In R/3, we have customers who are assigned to more than 1 ship-to party. The ship-to partner has a different number range from the sold-to party.

To link the sold-to party is easy. I just used PIDE to tie the account group '0001' to classification 'B'. However, I do not know whether I should do the same with account group '0002' (ship-to party). I tried replicating one ship-to party by linking account group '0002' to classification 'B' and CRM creates a customer with sold-to information maintained as well.

Is that the right way to do it? Or, do I have any other option?

✐ **ANSWER**

Yes, you describe the functionality properly. You can use the exclusion tab in BP to prevent all "ship-to's" from being allowed to act as a sold-to (manually or by writing your own enhancement).

The Customer in CRM (let's say "sold-to's") can have multiple ship-to addresses that do not have numbers in R/3. It depends on your long term strategy (what system will orders be entered to and where master data will be maintained). If CRM is the option, then it might be wise to "give up" your R/3 "ship-to's". But downside is no automatic way to do this. Again, do it manually or write your own enhancement.

☞ QUESTION 18

Mapping CRM BP to R/3

I have to map CRM business partners to the R/3 business partners.

How can I do this?

✍ ANSWER

Use PIDE Track. You can map R/3 to CRM and vice versa.

Other things you can do:

1. You can read the 'Best practices' for CRM for further familiarity with the subject.

2. Try transaction SMOEAC.

☞ QUESTION 19

Internet Sales

I have been working on CRM using the GUI and have not much knowledge in the Internet Sales functionality. My client wants the ability of the customer entering the specification/requirements wherein the system will return a list of possible products for his selection.

Is this possible? Can this requirement be met by using Guided Selling? Is there other ways apart from using Guided Selling?

✍ ANSWER

You can take a couple of approaches on this matter:

1. With the Product catalog, you can set up and assign product attributes to the product models and then use them as selection criteria in the product catalog.

2. With Product variants, you could build configurable products and use type matching with product variants to propose products based on cystic values.

3. Guided selling. Implementation of IPA and with the use of Knowledge base editor, looks pretty cool but may be a lot of set up depending on the number of products.

Option 1 would be much simpler and works well provided that there are no interdependencies between the attribute values, i.e. if you chose color = red, you can't have size=13;

An alternative approach:

There is a concept called Product Determination in Internet Sales of SAP CRM. Essentially, you would be in a position to attach some commonly used names to the CRM products and configure the same.

Please go through the relevant material on help.sap.com.

☞ **QUESTION 20**

Material Data flow from CRM to CDB

Does any one know how can we stop the material changes to flow from CRM to CDB?

✍ **ANSWER**

If you do not want to download all the materials from CRM to CDB then disable the MOBILEBRIDGE for Product download.

If you want it specific for particular material types then you need to enhance the Mobile Bridge Adapter not to map those material types.

☞ QUESTION 21

Pricing Conditions from SD to CRM

My client made a change in the discount conditions in SD and now they want that reflected on the CRM.

What I have been told is to run transaction R3AS, for some Objects, already specified by the client. Some examples of the Objects:

- DNL_CUST_SALES;
- ZDNL_CUST_A502;

Do I have to be careful with this Z object or is it the same?

After I load the Objects, how can I confirm the activity?

Is it necessary to restart IPC services so that the pricing will be reflected?

✍ ANSWER

You can use transaction R3AM1 to check that the customizing object was transferred.

When you update pricing or if the connection is broken between CRM and the IPC, you should always bounce the IPC manually

☞ QUESTION 22

CRM sales structure/data

I need help in creating CRM sales area data (distribution channel, division etc). I am not integrating with R/3 yet.

I set distance channel, division, sales organization, organizational data profile, determination rules et al in IMG.

However, it doesn't show up when I create BP as an organization.

How do I resolve this issue?

✍ ANSWER

Please check your organizational model if the scenario for sale is filled by the object you are using.

First, go to the BP which you created. Go to sold-to-party and in that one button, there will be an assigned sales area. Select that button then it will show all assigned sales area data. In there, select your sales area. It will immediately display related data below.

☞ QUESTION 23

Contact Person Replication from R/3 to CRM

I would like to confirm the concept that the contact person is replicated automatically when you input the customers from R/3 to CRM.

If that is the case, is there any way we can replicate the contact person with the same numbers as in the R/3 system using external number assignment?

If the contact persons get replicated to CRM through customer_main, then what is customer_rel used for?

Is it also true that contact persons get replicated using the object customer_rel?

✍ ANSWER

The answer to your first question is yes. Contact persons in R/3 are replicated to CRM through customer download (CUSTOMER_MAIN).

However, the original number does not seem considered, because there's no configuration possible in PIDE for contact persons. Moreover, the replicated number uses 'Standard Internal Number Range" in CRM.

If you still want to have the same number, you may think of further development in the configuration.

Lastly, 'CUSTOMER_REL' is used to replicate partner function data from R/3 to CRM.

☞ **QUESTION 24**

BDOC transfer of Sales Order from CRM to R/3 which function module

We have a standard CRM configuration - and are transferring BDOC's to our R/3 system via the BUS_TRANSACTION_MESG BDOC.

The problem we have is that our R/3 system is heavily modified (due to years of misuse and so many user exits etc). It seems that when sales orders are created via BDOC's they are not behaving in the same way as sales orders manually and directly in R/3 via transaction VA01.

What we would like to know is how to find out which function module / BAPI / RFC / Class is called by the CRM sales order BDOC on the R/3 server that actually begins the sales order creation transaction - so that we can perform some heavy duty debugging on it.

What is the function module (or if its a generated function module - how to find what the generated module is) that could assist us in our analysis of the problem?

✍ **ANSWER**

This can be resolved with a little help from SAP / OSS.

Just in case anyone else is having fun trying to debug the BDOC CRM to R/3 interface - SAP points to the following OSS note: 656823.

This details how to debug the BDOC interface (both inbound and outbound interfaces).

The function module name for the Sales order creation on the R/3 side is: BAPI_SALESDOCU_PROXY_UPLOAD.

☞ **QUESTION 25**

Trying to connect CRM and BW

I'm interested in downloading BW metadata to CRM.

In SMOBILEBW transaction I added the corresponding BW system and user links as well.

The problem is when I try to run the transactions CRM_RSA1, CRM_RRMX and CRM_RSMO; I'm getting the following error:

"RFC USER IS INVALID / NOT ALLOWED".

My RFC user is ALEREMOTE. I've tested the connections in transaction SM59 and they are functioning well.

How do I resolve this problem?

✍ **ANSWER**

The user ALEREMOTE had to be in dialog mode to function properly.

☞ QUESTION 26

Mobile Client Installation

I installed the Mobile client but there was an error saying that the user database couldn't be created.

What is the Username and Password for the installed client?

If I need to create a Username and Password, what do I need to do?

✍ ANSWER

If you have installed mobile client with demo database, ID/PW will be "crmuser/crm".

But, for an empty database, you have to assign SiteID and create ID/PW using 'SMOEAC'. Then, try to connect transactions in order to sync the data from CDB to the empty database. From there, you may log on successfully.

☞ QUESTION **27**

Pricing in CRM

Can we get price for the products by maintaining condition types in CRM without connecting to IPC?

✍ ANSWER

You can maintain condition records in CRM but you will need to IPC for pricing determination.

☞ **QUESTION 28**

CRM landing page

Could you tell me the transaction used for reaching the landing page for the web client from the GUI in CRM v4?

✍ **ANSWER**

If you are talking about BSP page, do the following:

1. /nSE80
2. Choose 'BSP Application'
3. Find 'CRM_BSP_FRAME'
4. Choose select.htm under 'Page with flow logic'

This page will guide you to choose one BSP application.

An alternative solution will be:

Open the WebClient from a browser, not the SAPGUI. As usual, the link depends on the server and ports you have it installed on. For example:

http://myserver:myports/sap/bc/bsp/sap/crm_ic/default. htm?sap-client=010

Now, if you were actually asking how to access the development components of the application, then the correct answer is SE80. Use BSP application CRM_IC.

☞ QUESTION **29**

Organization Model or Partners

I have a scenario where my client is using HR in R/3 and was distributing sales employees to CRM. They now wish to create complaints in CRM and want to determine an "approver" partner (which would then be assigned to an organization object) in the complaint document.

I think that this "approver" partner could be determined from the relationships on the organizational object BP or it could be determined from assignments in the organizational model.

I am not sure which option to suggest. The advantage of using related business partners is that the partner determination is easy. However, the maintenance is difficult. The same goes for the organizational model.

I am almost convinced that the ease of maintenance of the organization model is the clincher but I am unsure as to how this would be affected by organization model transports (we will maintain the org model in the development system and transport it into test and production). I hope that the organization model transports only move the organizational objects and not assigned employees. This is because we would have different assignments in dev/test/prod.

How does this behave?

Is there an existing critique or commentary on the partners/organization model choices?

✍ ANSWER

The Organization Model is a master data. It cannot be transported. There are function modules available in HR to move data between the different environments, e.g., development to production.

You can transport the Organization Model using the report RHMOVE30.

Section 2 CRM Functional

This section outline a list of commonly asked functional type questions.

These questions will range from the very basic to a more detailed answer with the software.

☞ **QUESTION 30**

Variant Configuration

Can you please help me out with the Variant Configuration in the SAP CRM?

I do know that it is configured in SAP MM but what is the use and effect of the Variant Configuration in CRM?

How is it done in CRM?

✑ **ANSWER**

Do the following steps:

1. Create your product models in R/3 (PME is a toy, avoid it like the plague).

2. Create a knowledge base.

3. Create a run time version.

Middleware object SCE distributes RTV to CRM.

IPC is used to configure the product during order entry.

☞ QUESTION 31

Order confirmation to be output from R/3 instead of CRM

Currently, the order confirmations are printed for all sales order in R/3. With the implementation of CRM, we will be creating SO in CRM. However, I just tested and found that the order confirmation is not printed when the SO is created-replicated in R/3. Is it possible to output the order confirmation from R/3?

What does "type of data exchange scenario" mean?

✍ ANSWER

For the first question, the answer is yes - you should be able to continue to issue order confirmation output from R/3.

For the second question: the available Data Exchange Scenarios are:

1. Standard scenario
2. Scenario X
3. Scenario Y
4. Scenario X+Y
5. Scenario Z
6. Scenario X+Z

Data exchange scenarios control how orders are distributed from CRM to R/3. These settings are made in the R/3 adapter and your options depend on which versions of R/3 and CRM you are working with.

For example, with scenario X, you can re-determine pricing and ATP and other stuff but still keep the "ownership" of the document as CRM. But if the document is changed in R/3 it becomes an R/3 document.

Each Scenario has it own limitations and issues but you need to choose one and understand how it will impact your users.

If you have not read OSS note 541113, I advise you to go through it as it will be very useful to you.

☞ QUESTION 32

Sales Order replication issue

I am currently working on data replication Mobile Sales application ->CRM -> R/3.

The issue is related to the Sales Order replication in CRM (or in Mobile Sales Application).

When I create a Sales Order in CMR and try to upload it on the R/3 system, an error appears and it is not uploaded on R/3. This is the error message that appears in the Sales Document after saving:

"An error has occurred in the system CRM while copying the document

TRNSMISSION LOG

Unknown object type 'BUS2000115' (Notification E RL 303)"

Furthermore, when a sales document is created in R/3 it is downloaded from R/3 to CRM but an error message appears as well:

"Unknown object type 'BUS2032'"

I have checked all transaction types in R/3 (copied from OS) and I created the transaction types in CRM copying from the TA one.

In the manner, I checked all item categories in R/3 (copied

from TAN) and I created the item categories in CRM copying from the TAN one.

What is the BOR object type's generation?

✍ ANSWER

The first place I would check is the existence of sales document types and item categories on both systems.

Also keep in mind that in R/3 there can be a translation of document type based on language i.e., an OR order type is really a TA. In CRM it should be a TA.

☞ QUESTION **33**

Resend BP record to R/3

Does anyone know any transaction code or program to resend a BP record to R/3?

An example is in a situation where I have not set the right link between CRM and R/3 via PIDE. So, when the BP created is created in CRM, it was not created in R/3 and somehow cannot find a BDOC to reprocess. In this case, I would need a facility to resend the record to R/3.

How can I remedy the situation?

✍ ANSWER

It's possible to resend BDOC'S from the display BDOC screen - smw01 and a few other middleware transactions. Although if setup correctly any deltas will get picked up by the middleware and sent automatically.

You can also try transaction CRMM_BUPA_MAP.

Enter the BP number and then click on the "send Business Partner data" button.

☞ QUESTION **34**

Mass Maintenance Functionality for BP

Does anyone know if there is any mass maintenance functionality for business partners?

We have had a sales representative leave the company and we want to swap him with his replacement as the "Employee Responsible" for his customers.

Is there an easy way to do this?

✍ ANSWER

I don't think there's a standard mass maintenance function. You can either use LSMW and the standard BAPI for changing relationships or you can build a tool yourself.

I have built a tool that uses a target group as a starting point. The users build a target group in the segment builder, and then they run a custom program that allows them to change certain fields for the entire BPs in that target group. This might serve your purpose as well.

☞ QUESTION **35**

Assigning or changing an Organizational Attribute

Can you change or assign an organizational attribute within the Organization Model functionality?

Can you change or assign organizational attribute within the configuration?

✍ ANSWER

Yes you can via the transaction code: OOATTRICUST. Please remember this is a core SAP configuration screen and the deletion of the attributes from here can not be recovered.

☞ QUESTION **36**

Deletion of Business Partner

I have a created a BP. For example, "test" as an organization. After that I feel that I should have created it with the same name as a person instead of an organization. But I couldn't find any way to delete the business partner because whenever I create with the same name as a person, it says that the business partner with the same name exists. Thus, I want to delete the BP. No documents have been created yet with this BP.

How do I do this?

✍ ANSWER

Use transactions BUPA_PRE_DA and BUPA_DEL to do this.

☞ QUESTION 37

BP creation Mobile Sales

When we are trying to save a business partner in mobile sales the following error is reflected:

"Error Occurred in processing: no territory assigned to user"

However, if we click the ok button, the BP is still getting saved.

How do we get rid of the error message constantly reflected and resolve this issue?

✍ ANSWER

The system entry TERRMGMTFLAG in the MSY should be set to 0 to deactivate the territory management.

- Go to MSY " Cross Components Settings " Choice Fields;
- Select TERRMGMTFLAG;
- Set value to 0;
- Save;
- To load your settings to the other mobile clients, do a Connecting Transaction;

☞ **QUESTION 38**

Error in processing Quotation in CRM

I am working on a leasing quotation in CRM 5.0. After saving the quotation, when I try to open the quotation for further processing, the system is generating a message "Document is being distributed - changes are not possible". As a result of this message I am not able to open the quotation in Change mode.

How do resolve this issue?

✑ **ANSWER**

The message implies that you are replicating to R/3. Check SMQ1, SMQ2 in both R/3 & CRM to see if BDOC are hung.

Typically, quotations in CRM are not distributed to R/3 until they are converted to order status at the item and/or header.

It also sounds like your document or item categories are not configured correctly. Your quotation or at least some of the items on your quotation regard it as an order. Check for errors now before it complicates matters later.

☞ QUESTION **39**

Prices in the CRM Product Master

I know SD pricing from before, and know the conditional technique but when I look in CRM it seems like there are prices in the product master.

I am not sure if this is true in all CRM scenarios (we use service).

In SD, there are no prices in the material master (other than cost) but in CRM there seems to be one. When are these prices used and how do they correlate to the normal pricing technique?

✍ ANSWER

This works similar to how pricing is carried out in r/3. If the condition as shown in the product and as configured in CRM is relevant, then it will be applied.

If you are retrieving you're pricing from r/3 then you should not maintain conditions in CRM.

In R/3 there is a set of transactions used to maintain pricing condition records. The transaction depends on the type of condition object and change created.

In CRM there is also a transaction for centrally maintaining any condition record: /sapcnd/gcm.

Also, condition types can be configured to be displayed and or maintained through the relevant object.

In your system the condition maintenance object for products includes one or more condition types. This is causing them to be displayed through the product master. But the condition records are not actually part of the product master records.

☞ **QUESTION 40**

IC Webclient in IDES via SAP Menu

When I click on the IC Webclient in IDES via SAP Menu > Interaction Center > Interaction Center Webclient, I get the result in a pop-up window asking for "<Host><Port><Path> <File>".

In real time projects, do you also get the same results? If so, do you enter the address too?

✍ **ANSWER**

We do not have an IDES system, but have a demo system which we use for elaborating demos for our customers. What I suggest is for you to read on the IC Webclient Cookbook. It is available on service.sap.com!

☞ QUESTION 41

Access of IC Webclient

How do you access IC Webclient interface at the start of implementation process in SAP CRM?

✍ ANSWER

Architecture and Technology an ABAP Workbench with an Overview of the Object Navigator Transaction code SE80.

To access the IC Webclient you will need to know the URL:

You can check this with Transaction code SE80 (object navigator). Next select for example the BSP Application CRM_IC.

Select 'pages with Flow Logic 'and double click on the page "default.htm". Select on the right hand side of the screen the Tab Page "properties". There you will find the URL!!

VIA Transaction code SM59 you can check the hostname settings!

☞ **QUESTION 42**

Campaigns/Opportunity Management

We would like to run a campaign where all customers within a certain grouping will be sent information about a new product. We have not configured campaigns or opportunities as of yet and we do not know how to best proceed with it.

Our example would be something like this:

To select customers based on Industry code:

To make Industry and Industry code from OLTP available on CRM under Classification/Industry Sector and under Identification/Industries;

Is this possible? Which is better to use - a campaign or an opportunity? Or, are they interlinked?

Are there any good documentation regarding setting up campaigns etc.?

✍ **ANSWER**

You should realize that for campaign management, you have to define a specific communication media (like email, phone, letter, fax, lead or activity generation and so on), relevant transaction types, marketing attributes, data sources, attribute list and target groups.

You could also start doing the following things:

Step 1: In customizing you will link certain transaction types.

For example: a lead type to your defined communication medium 'Lead generation'.

In your case, you want to send information out to a group of customers.

In that case I suggest a communication medium like "e-mail' which has a communication method 'internet mail (SMTP)' and Transaction type 0005 - outgoing email.

Step 2: you can create marketing attributes (you can define whatever marketing attribute you want):

- You can create marketing attributes on a business partner level (transaction code CRMD_PROF_CHAR); then, you can assign one or more of those attributes to an attribute set (transaction code CRMD_PROF_TEMPL);

Remark: In your case you will base yourself on an existing field "industry sector" so it is not really necessary to create a new marketing attribute.

Here, you will need to assign marketing attributes to the relevant business partners if you are following this strategy.

To do so, you will go into Business partner maintenance (transaction code BP) and on the tab page 'Marketing attributes ' you first assign an Attribute set, and next can maintain the relevant marketing attributes.

Step 3: You will create a new data source and Attribute List.

Transaction code = CRMD_MKTDS;

Here, you need to choose which origin type you will be using for this data source:

- Attribute set (as explained in step 2);
- BW Cube (can be used if you are using BW, and have a query defined that creates a list of all business partners with a certain industry code). You can export your 'result list' as target group to the CRM system;
- Infoset --this is probably the thing you need in your case. Create a new infoset for the relevant tables;
- External list Management;

Step4: Create an attribute list based on one or more data sources and select the relevant fields from those data sources for filtering purposes.

Step5: Create a new target group in the Segment builder (Transaction code CRMD_MKTSEG) and use the attribute list you created before.

☞ QUESTION 43

CRM MARKETING: SEGMENT BUILDER

On the CRM-MARKETING-SEGMENT BUILDER:

We need to be able to create Target Groups using the 'OR' criteria. Unfortunately SAP seems to offer only the 'AND' (keep) and 'NOT' (split) criteria. This is visible when making drag & drop from the Components Area (left side, list of attributes) into the Staging Area of the Segment Builder (right side, where Target Groups are created).

How could we achieve a target group that would be inclusive? For example: either male or female customers?

✍ ANSWER

Create sex as an attribute and then import both into the attribute list and make them active as multiple values.

If you drag filters on to Staging area, by default it will be OR Operation.

For example: You have 2 attributes and have created filters for them. Once you drag those filters on to the staging area, two profiles will appear. If you create Target Group for Profile Set then the system will perform "OR" operation between those two profiles.

Also, if you combine two Targets Groups you can do an 'OR' condition:

- Create a Profile with each of the Attributes you need;
- Build the Target Group for each profile;
- Combine the Target Groups to obtain an or condition;

☞ QUESTION 44

Profile, Profile Sets, Target Groups - relationships

My question is:

Is there any relationship existing between: Profile, Profile Sets and Target Groups?

I am interested in knowing if a Profile is a subset of Profile Set, which in turn is a subset of Target Group.

✍ ANSWER

First of all, I advise you to check the SAP HELP:

http://help.sap.com/saphelp_crm40sr1/helpdata/en/db/58963eac416f01e10000000a114084/frameset.htm; check the Folder "Target Group Creation". There you have explanations on Profile Sets, Profiles and Target Groups.

A profile set consists of individual marketing segments - profiles, target groups and other profile sets - which were modeled together and which are to be interpreted together.

A profile is a semantic description of a target group in terms of the selection criteria used to create such a group.

All of the selection criteria within the profile must be met before a business partner matches the profile, that is, the attributes within the profile are linked together as "and" conditions.

A target group is a list of business partners that have been combined for a specific marketing activity. In Segment Builder, target groups can be created both by executing the selection conditions for a marketing profile or independently of the profile, for example by importing a list of business partners from an external system. It is also possible to select target groups in the BW System (transaction rstg_bupa), and then to create them from there directly in CRM.

In Mobile Sales, a target group can contain business partners and contact persons, depending on the chosen selection criteria.

Target groups can have one of two statuses: active and inactive, whereby only active target groups can be used in the application.

Remark: you can create a target group directly, by manually adding business partners for example in a target group. In that case there is no link to an existing profile or profile set.

I also can give you the table links that I investigated on a previous project:

Example:

1) You created a Target group based on a profile set (without a profile link):

CRMD_MKTTG_SET_H-GUID = CRMD_MKTTG_TG_H-SET-SET_GUID

Example 2) Create target group based on Profile:

LINK Profile Set with Profile:

CRMD_MKTTG_SET_H-GUID = CRMD_MKTTG_PF_H-SET_GUID

LINK Profile with Target Group

CRMD_MKTTG_PF_H-GUID = CRMD_MKTTG_TG_H-PROF_GUID

The Text tables have the same name as the Table Names above, but replace the _H with _T

☞ QUESTION 45

Campaign thru Email

I have a query on Campaigns done through email. When I send email to the customer and the mail box is full, the mail gets bounced.

How can I be able to monitor when the mail is bounced? Do I get any confirmation on this or is there any other way to check the bounced mails? Where exactly is it stored?

✍ ANSWER

If the mailbox is full you will receive the bounced back email in your inbox. It will be difficult for you to trap all the mails. You have to write one report for this. However, you can also check it out in SCOT Transaction code YAR.

In fact, in the CRM 5.0 release (or also in the CRM 4.0 release, but in that case you need to have installed the CRMIS - CRM industry solution extension pack) you have the ERMS functionality (Email Response Management System).

This is a very useful tool for handling emails. You can setup routing, rules for handling email, content analysis, bouncing etc.

For more information on email monitoring, log on to www. service.sap.com and read a bit on this subject. create the BP.

☞ QUESTION 46

Assign a sales group to multiple sales offices

We are on CRM 4.0. With this version, we are supposed to be able to assign a sales group to multiple sales offices. I've executed the step in configuration to switch our organization model to the Enhanced Backend Integration Model and then tried the assignment again. No luck. I didn't accomplish what I set out to do.

How do I accomplish the assignment of the sales group to multiple sales offices?

Do you know if there's a program or transaction that will delete the Organization Model? You can manually delete it, but the previous assignments are still there. Is there any other way to do it?

✍ ANSWER

Try looking at the function tab. This is where you can make the assignments.

With regards your second question, you need to delete the previous assignments. Run the transaction code to perform that function.

Meanwhile, in the sales office tab in ppoma, you can add the sales organization to the settings on the lower half of the screen. (Change the layout and add the sales organization). Here you can add the sales organization.

There is also a note where you can do the following to help

with your task:

    0001 * *
    0002 * *

So you don't have to assign to everyone (assuming you use enhanced model).

In case you are interested, the problem with the sales office and sales group not appearing for assignment in the BP and sales transaction – this is due to buffering. The scenario SALE was not set up for buffering. In this case, you need to turn on the buffer in table T77OMATTR and also run the refresh buffer program HRBCI_ATTRIBUTES_BUFFER_UPDATE.

☞ QUESTION 47

System asking for service organization when creating task from activities

I have just installed the BP for CRM and testing out the Activity Management transaction by following the BPP. However, when I created the task from the activity, it was asking for service organization. The configuration does not include an organization determination profile.

Is it because an organization profile is not maintained and why it started asking for a service organization?

Also, I do not quite understand the intention of leaving that organization profile field blank. I have done similar a installation in a separate system and for the same create task transaction, the organization is not required at all.

Why is this problem happening and how do I resolve the issue?

✍ ANSWER

If you are not using the automatic organization determination procedure (either you have not set this up yourself, or are using the standard procedures) for a specific transaction type such as TASK, then you should leave the field BLANK.

At this moment, if you would check the transaction type you have defined, you probably will have something maintained for the Org Determination profile. You more than likely have both the "Sales and Service" active on the profile for the

TASK.

Out of the box, both Sales and Service will be active (perhaps because you made a copy of a standard transaction for task, such as the TA type 1003 or 1004).

So my advice is, if you don't use it, just delete this procedure on Transaction type level in customizing to avoid complications.

☞ **QUESTION 48**

Business Transactions, Types, Categories

I have a query on
- Business Transactions
- Business Transaction Types
- Business Transaction Categories

The question is:

What is subset of what? That means:

- Is Transaction subset of Transaction Types, which in turn subset of Categories?
- What is the correct relationship between those three?

✍ **ANSWER**

In your CRM system you have first of all Business Transaction Categories:

This can be of the types:

- activity (BUS2000126)
- lead (BUS2000108)
- task (BUS2000125)
- .....

Next, per Leading Transaction CATEGORIE, you can have one or more Transaction Types

SAP Delivers several standard transaction types per transaction category (you can see this in customizing)!!

FOR CRM system: IMG--> Customer Relationship management--> Transactions--> Basic settings--> Define Transaction types

for example, for a Business Activity, you will find back:

0000 Business Activity
0001 Sales Call
0002 Incoming Call
0003 Outgoing Phone Call
0004 Incoming E-Mail
0005 Outgoing E-Mail
and so on!!!

Last, you have the transactions!
In fact, a transaction in this case would be a business transaction!!

For example;

You create a business activity of the Type "sales call" in your system!

In that case the system will save this transaction as a number!

In the table CRMD_ORDERADM_H, after creating for example a standard transaction of the type 'sales call", you will find this back by entering the Number of the transaction! Or you can just look up all transactions by "process type", which in that case would be '0001'.

☞ QUESTION 49

Questionnaire in Activity

I've activated a questionnaire in an opportunity without a problem, but the activity is causing me fits. I've added the three item categories. In looking at the documentation, it says I need to create an activity journal as well, with an Activity Journal Template Type of "questionnaire". According to the documentation, this is a standard (SAP provided) type, but it doesn't exist in any of our systems, including IDES.

How can CRM implement statistical function through a questionnaire in Activity?

✍ ANSWER

You do not need an activity journal to implement questionnaires in activities.

You should first create a questionnaire/Survey via the Survey suite builder. (T-code CRM_SURVEY_SUITE).

Make SURE that you create it in the folder "activities" since that is where you want to use it.

Next, in customizing you need to configure the right settings:

IMG--> CRM--> Transactions--> Settings for activities--> Questionnaires:

- Define determination for questionnaires (contact or Task)

- Define determination criteria for questionnaires.

Finally, make sure that your Survey is "Activated".

☞ QUESTION 50

Finding Actual Activity Dates

When I load transaction CRMD_BUS2000126 (Maintain Activities) and load an activity, I see the actual start and end dates. However, I wish to put these into a SAP Query Report. I can't seem to find them in the system.

Does anybody know the underlying tables where the actual dates are stored for a CRM Activity?

✍ ANSWER

The actual activity dates may be in the table SCAPPT.

You have to take the GUID from the CRMD_ORDERADM_H table and feed it into the CRMD_LINK table (Transaction - Set - Link) which gives you a GUID which in turn can be used to find the correct record in the table SCAPPT.

☞ QUESTION 51

Duration for activity can't be changed in CIC

When an activity is created in CIC I need to change the date and time. Date and time for the activity is to be set in the future. But when you save the activity, the date and time will be overwritten by the actual date and time.

Why is the date and time overwritten in CIC and how can this be resolved?

The problem doesn't occur when you create an activity with transaction. For example: CRMD_ORDER.

What's the difference between CIC and CRMD_ORDER?

✍ ANSWER

For problems in this area, define a date rule which sets a two day duration to calculate a future planned end date. However, this is overridden when you create the activity in the web IC.

The XML rules which are used in the date calculation are not called when you create the activity through the Web IC, hence they are overridden. Still, have an OSS note logged and waiting for a formal response from SAP.

An alternative approach would be to create an implementation of the Business Add-In CRM_ APPOINTMENT_BADI. This BADI contains a method CRM_APPOINTMENT_MERGE, the signature of which has access to a structure CS_APPOINTMENT_BADI; this structure contains the field TIMESTAMP_TO which is the 'Planned to' date field. The planned end date can then be controlled and determined when the BADI is called.

☞ QUESTION 52

Recording for creating Follow-Up Activity

I'm trying to create a recording for follow-up activities.

The manual process I use is clicking on the PLUS ICON on the Activity Document (used for creating follow-up activities). It gives a List of Business Activity Types. From there, I select the Relevant Activity Type.

During the recording process, it does not get the value of the PLUS ICON, and therefore I'm not able to create a follow-up activity document using BDC or SCAT.

How could I create the follow-up activities automatically?

✍ ANSWER

You can play around with the function BAPI_ACTIVITYCRM_ CREATEMULTI.

I have used it to download all the activities from the legacy system and I believe you can create a follow-up transaction if you populate the DOCUMENT_FLOW structure.

I am sure this would facilitate your purpose.

☞ QUESTION 53

Statuses

After setting the system status to Completed, where can I select back to In Process if necessary? I am trying to find the settings.

✍ ANSWER

You can find the settings in transaction within the IMG.

You can also try transaction "BSVW".

☞ QUESTION 54

Adding partner to activity

I am trying to add a new partner to an existing activity using the function module BAPI_ACTIVITYCRM_CHANGEMULTI.

When the HEADER, HEADERX, PARTNER, PARTNERX tables are filled, the PARTNER table is filled with the following fields:

PARTNER_FCT = '0000022'
PARTNER_NO = '4000000' (Existing BP)
NO_TYPE = 'BP'
DISPLAY_TYPE = 'BP'
REF_PARTNER_HANDLE = '0001'

The activity description is changed (for testing), but I get the following error in RETURN table: 'Referenced object type (PARTNER) not allowed'.

What did I do wrong? How should I use this function to add a partner to activity?

✍ ANSWER

When you use the function module BAPI_ACTIVITYCRM_ CHANGEMULTI to change an existing activity I believe you should give the activity GUID as a parameter instead of the handle parameter, it should be something like this:

PARTNER-REF_GUID = '4296CA77C8D737DBE10000000 A65647A' (CRMD_ORDERADM_H-GUID)
REF_PARTNER_HANDLE = '0000'

PARTNER_FCT = '0000022'
PARTNER_NO = '4000000' (Existing BP)
NO_TYPE = 'BP'
DISPLAY_TYPE = 'BP'
PARTNER-MAINPARTNER = 'X'.

This code will help you to add a new BP in the activity created, if you need to change one existing business partner in the activity for another BP you need to use the fields call partner-ref*.

☞ **QUESTION 55**

Internet email address

Where can I find the internet mail addresses for Business Partners stored?

Is it in table ADR6?

✍ **ANSWER**

In table ADR6 you have the SMTP. However, in table BUT020 you have the connection between the Business Partner and the address (Field ADDRNUMBER).

In table ADR6 you also have the Internet Mail (Field SZA1_ D0100-SMTP_ADDR in transaction BP).

☞ QUESTION 56

Common Divisions

I have a problem with pricing due to the use of common divisions in R/3.

How do I set up common divisions in CRM?

✍ ANSWER

If you are talking about sales area bundling, there is a step in the IMG where you can download common sales areas. The transaction is CRMD_DOWNLOAD_SB.

This is downloaded from R/3 using transaction CRMD_ DOWNLOAD_SB.

Take a look at the documentation in the IMG CRM>Masterdata>Org Management> Transfer commonly used.

Transaction CRMD_DOWNLOAD_SB populates tables SMOTVKOS, SMOTVKOV and SMOTV which contain the pointers for common sales area for conditions, customers, etc.

☞ QUESTION 57

MWST Determination Error

In our scenario we created a complaint document in CRM, and based upon the net value, a credit memo request or debit memo request is created through an action.

The credit/debit should be automatically distributed to R/3. However, we have started to get a pricing error telling us that the MWST condition is missing. This is stopping the BDOC from being processed in CRM.

This never used to be a problem. R/3 used to calculate the tax and send it back to the document in CRM.

I have checked all of the replication objects and the PITC/ PITM settings. Everything seems to be ok.

Why are we getting this problem now? What is the solution?

✍ ANSWER

The problem may have occurred during the replication process.

Check if somebody within your business partners and organizational units got out of sync. Then go back and check throughout the process again.

☞ QUESTION 58

Copy multiple service contracts to one

I'm developing a BADI action (the normal way through activity transactions etc in SPRO) to call a screen where the user can select multiple service contracts which contents should be copied into one (including correct document flow).

It works for one contract (of course, as in Standard), but I can't make it work for a multiple contract. I'm using functions CRM_ORDER_MAINTAIN and CRM_ORDER_SAVE right now.

How should they be called?

✍ ANSWER

This a short description of the solution:

- Use method lc_action_execute->get_ref_object to pick up the GUID you are creating or changing (ORDERADM_H)

- Use a new screen for picking products from different existing contracts. Collect them in an internal table.

- call CRM_ORDER_MAINTAIN: use structures IT_ PRODUCT_I, IT_CUSTOMER_I (for my own EEWB fields), CT_ORDERADM_H (initial when calling!), CT_ ORDERADM_I, CT_INPUT_FIELDS and CT_DOC_FLOW.

After that leave the action BADI and get back to Standard transaction CRMD_ORDER. Now you can see the service contract has one or many product items + document flow filled on header + item level. When pressing save in Transaction, the service contract is stored on the DB.

The key is just to use CRM_ORDER_MAINTAIN in the correct way (to store order data to the buffer, will be visible on screen as well), the rest is taken cared of by the transaction itself. Key fields in the structures are for instance ORDERADM_I-HEADER, and REF_GUID/GUID in all structures.

CRM_ORDER_SAVE is done in the transaction later.

☞ QUESTION 59

Reading HTML Documents in Business Workplace

We have mails coming into the Business Workplace of SAP CRM, in HTML Format. We are supposed to read those emails and convert them to Activities. The HTML mails come in with tags (sample below). We are having problems in executing our program.

What needs to be done to avoid mails with HTML Tags?

Example: Mail with HTML Tags:

Ticket No. : 175229
Type Of Feedback : 5
Sub Type : Order Related
CSR Email : shoppingorderstatus@time sgroup.com
User ID : scameron
User Name : Scott Cameron
User Mobile : 4035551212
User Email : scameron@sapcookbooks.com
Order No. :
Activity No :

: Message : Hi, I just wanted to know whether you can ship my Order in the Calgary. Please confirm that you have a partener courier agency that can ship my order on time.

I will be thankful.

Regards,

Customer Ar

We would like the mails to come in this manner:

Ticket No. : 175229
Type Of Feedback : 5

Sub Type : Order Related
CSR Email : ABC@email.com,ca
User ID : scameron
User Name : Scott Cameron
User Mobile : 4035551212
User Email : scameron@email.com,ca
Order No. :
Activity No :
Message : Hi, I just wanted to know whether you can ship my
Order in the Calgary, Please confirm that you have a partner
courier agency that can ship my order on time.

✍ ANSWER

Check the following entry:

Table: SXPARAMS;

Parameter: MULTIPART/ALTERNATIVE;

Value: Text or Value: HTML;

With this you should be able to see HTML mails in SBWP.

You cannot, however, execute email in SBWP.

☞ QUESTION 60

Sales Data in Product

We are trying to maintain sales data (Sales Organization, Distribution Channel) for the product of type 'Material' in transaction commpr01. However, these sales area fields along with the buttons (Assign, Copy) are grayed out.

Does anyone know what's the reason behind this and how could this be changed?

✐ ANSWER

You have to maintain the distribution chain and division data under organizational configuration in IMG.

Even though you transferred sales organization data from R/3 using copy function, Material Master is not relevant to them.

You can use 'DNL_CUST_S_AREA' object to download this data from R/3. However, you have to improvise a little to use this object via M/W => please, find a note with 'DNL_CUST_S_AREA'.

Another option is for you to maintain it manually.

☞ QUESTION 61

Action condition dependency on the reason code

I have set up a number of actions for activities wherein the condition involves checking the reason code within the activity. The condition works fine. However, when I enter a result code in the activity the action is deactivated because there are now two entries in the code table and the system seems to get confused even though the reason and result codes belong to two different code catalogues.

I have 'trend' putting in additional logic in the condition to take account of the result code but to no avail.

How do I get around this problem and resolve it?

✍ ANSWER

The reasons and results are both implemented with the help of the same sub-object - SERVICE_OS.

You will have to include both Status Reason and Activity Reason in the condition. Depending on which is the triggering reason you will have to use the operator 'CE' on one and '=' on the other. Play around with it until it works the way you want it to.

☞ QUESTION 62

Assigning user status to system

I am working on a status profile wherein after assigning some controls to the status, I want to assign the system status to it as well.

I am simulating the same and it is going fine and saving in the new variant as well. However, upon testing that, it doesn't seem to get through. I logged off and on again, but it is behaving erratically.

What is the appropriate process of assigning the user status to the system status?

✍ ANSWER

In Transaction/CRMBS02, go to the transaction controls:

Menu ----> extras --> status simulation;

Simulate the same with object CPG (campaign) and create a variant. Shuttle between user status and system status and see the simulated view until it is perfect.

Then go back to CRMBS02 and position cursor at the user status. Go to menu ---> environment --> system status. Upon reaching the TRANSACTION/BS23 in the transaction control, double click on status until you reach the screen.

Menu----> Environment---> Transactions takes you to Transaction/ BS33.

Use T Code BS22 for the change mode.

The other option is to customize the Transaction control.

Go to APPR stats and then AM11 (Approve) Business Transaction option. This leads to APPR (I1809) status set. Set that as next TRANSACTION in CRMBS02.

Technical

Since the system is an amalgamation between functional and technical, some question may be viewed as a more functional.

This point of view usually depends on your SAP experience. I have just tried to group these logically depending on the level of technical knowledge needed to solve the questions. Some of these functional types of questions will need a technical skill to implement.

☞ QUESTION 63

CRM tables

Can anybody provide the details of the frequently used CRM tables?

✍ ANSWER

The frequently used tables are:

1. CRMD*
2. CRMC*

☞ QUESTION **64**

Transaction codes

Is there an existing list with the most important transaction codes?

✍ ANSWER

All transactions can be found in se93.

You can also do the following:

Click the SAP menu open, you have folders like:

- activities
- marketing
- external list management
- business partner segmentation and so on....

In every folder there are Transactions available. To know the T-code for these transactions you have to put on the technical names.

You can do this in the MENU:

Extra--> Settings--> flag "Display technical names".

☞ QUESTION 65

List of BADIs

Where can we find the list of BADI's dependent on the application we do in userexits?

✍ ANSWER

You can find them in transaction /SPRO. Find the folder first. When the configuration of the application selective is done and if there is any, you will find the BADI's assigned to them including the documentation.

You can also search the BADI's via se18:

Press the F4 button to search;

Use the button INFOSYSTEM OR SAP-applications;

If you are looking for a CRM related BadI you can use as an example the infosystem button and type in:

CRM* (in definition name);

You will then get a list of all CRM related BADI's.

☞ QUESTION 66

IPC User Exits

I have modified the "pricingUserExits.java" file (and the others) to include a new pricing routine.

I have two questions though:

1. How can I compile it locally to check that there are no syntax errors?

2. How do I get it onto the IPC?

✍ ANSWER

You can use the eclipse function to create a project and build/ compile your changes. In the build path you can include all the JAR files from the IPC that will be needed to successfully compile it.

Once you have your compiled class file, you can then drop it on the server IPC/lib/userexits directory and stop and restart the IPC server and dispatcher services. server.

☞ QUESTION 67

Converting Sales Orders from R/3 with Sales Office & Group

I am trying to decide on the best way to convert our Sales Order's from R/3 to CRM because the Sales Office and Sales Group are being used in R/3. Basically, we do not want to use the sales office and sales group anymore in CRM. However, the sales office and sales group are assigned in all the existing customers and Sales Order's in R/3.

Thus, I have a problem replicating the Sales Order's over to CRM because the system does not seem to be able to determine the Responsible Organization Unit even though the sales organization and sales district are populated successfully. Based on the determination rule that I have set (which determines the organization unit by BP), the system should be able to determine the organization that is assigned to the BP (attribute maintained in the organizational structure). It should pull out the BP (sold-to) and then be able to scan the organizational structure for PARTNER attribute that includes BP.

My question is, shouldn't the system determine the sales organizational structure that has the 'Object Permitted in Organization' indicator turned on and the attribute maintained?

It seems to me that the system is also taking the sales office and sales group in consideration when trying to determine the organizational unit.

Can anyone please clarify my understanding of the use of the determination rule 10000148?

✍ ANSWER

You can go to your organizational definition and mark sales office & group as 'not mandatory'. The organizational definition is assigned to the transaction type. Your sales orders should not require those values.

Organizational data determination is not carried out during this process. The organizational data is copied from the R/3 order. Review the settings for data exchange scenarios.

Never consider BOR objects with regards to middleware. I have worked with them in launching R/3 transactions from within the IC in CRM but I can't imagine how they apply to this issue.

☞ QUESTION 68

How to lock the transaction screen

We have a scenario. In CRMD_ORDER, I am viewing the sales order. The users click the change button. In change mode, I have to check for some condition for status. If the condition is true, I need to lock the transaction (i.e. to stop the user from further editing the transaction). Is there any function module which i can use to do it?

✍ ANSWER

This may be possible through a BADI implementation for definition CRM_SALES_CHECK. In standard CRM it should be "locked" the transaction once already in change mode and can not be accesses by another user until you save or exit the transaction.

☞ QUESTION **69**

CRM-on error, transaction shouldn't save and return to screen

CRM-Sales Contract, when an error occurs, the messages get collected in the log and transaction gets saved (a document number is created). I need to display that message in the status bar (at the bottom) and stop CRM from creating a document (just like we do in R/3, without line item data, a document does not get created). I know that in CRM, the standard is to collect the messages but is it also a standard to create the transaction even though there are errors?

I need to keep displaying error messages until all are resolved and then save/create the document. How can I do this?

✍ ANSWER

That is how CRM functions. All business transactions can be saved regardless of the status. The status (errors) will stop transactions from processing further (-->R/3) through the system.

☞ QUESTION 70

Customization of Generic Interaction Layer Know-how

What does "Customization of Generic Interaction Layer Know-how" mean? Is it necessary for a functional consultant to know about them?

This is what I have encountered so far: "BSP_WD_WORKBENCH - IC Webclient Workbench & CRMV_GENIIL - Customization of Generic Interaction Layer".

✍ ANSWER

BSP_WD_WORKBENCH is used to create in an easier way a new BSP Applications, BSP pages, controllers and stuff like that.

During the implementation of the IC Webclient at a previous customer however, we did all the necessary changes via SE80 (object navigator).

This transaction is available from release CRM 4.0 when you have the Industry Extension pack installed, or from release CRM. 5.0.

CRMV_GENIL is for changing the Generic interface layer. It is very complex and it is best not to change anything without thorough knowledge. The best thing to do is to follow the CR410 course first. Or, at least read and understand the IC Webclient cookbook.

☞ **QUESTION 71**

How delete the address in CRM

How can we delete duplicate addresses in the CRM Address Tab?

✍ **ANSWER**

This might help you:

BAPI_BUPA_ADDRESS_REMOVE;

An alternative would be:

FM : ADDRESS_DELETE;

☞ **QUESTION 72**

CRM error: 'Pricing data for partner 8000116 could not be found'

I am having a problem while creating Sales Order in CRM. I am getting this error:

"Pricing data for partner 8000116 could not be read"

How do I resolve this issue?

✍ **ANSWER**

Check if that BP is assigned to any sales area and if it has all the requirements filled like currency, payment, etc.

Also make sure the IPC is configured correctly.

Then, check to see if organization data is determined. Remember that data like currency and pricing procedure type is distribution chain specific, so organization unit must be determined before pricing data can be determined.

Check if the Customer pricing procedure is maintained on the Business partner (sold-to party role) on sales area data and tab page billing.

☞ QUESTION 73

Unable to use condition PR00

I am using CRM 4.0 and am trying to connect it to an R/3 system. I have already done the initial load with success.

But now I am creating a material in the R/3 system and theme assignment to the PR00 pricing condition. The mapping is done but the material doesn't contain that specific pricing condition. When I try to assign it to the material, there is no record available for selection.

What is happening here and how do I resolve this?

✍ ANSWER

1. Pricing makes the input values sales area, partner procedure and document pricing procedure available to condition technique.

2. The system determines the pricing procedure dependent on sales area, partner procedure and document pricing procedure.

3. The system reads the first condition type of the pricing procedure and determines the assigned access sequence.

4. This step, together with the following steps, is repeated for each condition type on the pricing procedure.

5. The system reads the access sequence with the condition tables.

6. The sequence of the condition tables forms the search strategy for determining the individual condition records. Each condition table contains the field combinations according to which the system should search in the condition records.

For example: business partner– product price.

The system searches for valid condition records for the condition tables. If the system does not find a valid condition record for the first condition table, it carries on and searches for a condition record for the next condition table.

Once the system has found a valid condition record for a condition table, it makes the result available to pricing in the form of prices and discounts.

If the search procedure contains more than one condition type, the system repeats the search for condition records for each condition type.

It also functions the same if you offer a customer a special price for a product, and create a special condition record specifically for this customer and this product. In the pricing procedure the first condition type is the 'Price'. The access sequence for this condition type specifies that the system first search for a customer-specific price (field combination business partner – product – price. In this way, the system can automatically determine the customer-specific price in the business transaction, and calculate the total price using the quantity ordered.

☞ QUESTION 74

Changing a field group in a PCUI screen

I would like to make some fields mandatory in a PCUI screen. I know which field group I need to modify but otherwise I'm not sure how to proceed from there.

Where can I find any useful documentation to enable me to resolve this problem?

✍ ANSWER

My suggestion is that you create your own view and then copy the fields in your field groups to your newly created view. This way you can easily take out and modify the fields without affecting PCUI applications that are running without a view.

If you want to make a field mandatory, just check the 'mandatory' check box of the specified field in your view. Of course you need to make sure that your application is then using the view in EP or ICWC.

☞ **QUESTION 75**

Problem creating BP from LSMW using IDOC

I am trying to insert a business partner using LSMW and the IDOC type CRMXIF_PARTNER_SAVE_M, but I am getting the following errors:

"Error status 'A ' calling validation service
Message no. CRMXIF_COMMON010

Validation error occurred: Module CRM_BUPA_MAIN_VAL ,
BDOC BUPA_MAIN .
Message no. SMW3018

Date / / contains invalid characters
Message no. S5011

Partner (...): the following errors occurred
Message no. BUPA_MW_EXCHANGE010"

Please note that I did not enter anything at all in the date field.

I also tried to directly input values from WE19 in that IDOC type and got the same result.

How do I successfully create the Business Partner using LSMW and the IDOC type referred to?

✍ ANSWER

Try filling the date with a '/' to indicate that it is empty. This should work for you.

☞ QUESTION 76

How to write some thing on logon screen

I want to write some information on logon screen of SAP.

How should I proceed?

✍ ANSWER

Have a look at OSS-message 205487. This will clarify matters for you and provide a detailed step by step process.

☞ **QUESTION 77**

About the authorization for Lead, opportunity, activity

I have a problem about authorization.

How can I control the authorization in maintaining business transaction that use the Sales org / channel / sales office / sales group?

✍ **ANSWER**

You can use the authorization object CRM_ORD_OE for that issue.

☞ QUESTION 78

Configuration Changes after Go-Live

When you perform a replication in CRM development there is no transport, so it's not like you can transport the configuration change up to test and production from there.

How do you deal with configuration changes in R/3 after you have gone live in CRM?

Should I re-run the replication for the customizing in development, test and production?

✍ ANSWER

Here is my favorite tip:

In CRM, I use table SE16 SMOFTABLES. When there is an R/3 configuration change you need to see what table was transported. You can get from SE10 the details. Then I use SMOFTABLES to add the R/3 table name. That will tell you what object you need to replicate (assuming it can be replicated, order types & item categories have to be configured in CRM & R/3).

☞ QUESTION 79

CRM security - looking for guidance

My company is just beginning a CRM project. I have familiarized myself with the Security Guide for SAP CRM, and I am looking for feedback in a couple of areas.

Is there a methodology behind collecting and documenting authorization information that the end users will require for various CRM modules? Have you utilized templates or processes that helped with this in your projects?

Do you have any wisdom to share regarding things to beware of, tips, best practices, etc?

How much user administration does a CRM solution typically require?

✎ ANSWER

I did authorizations setup in several projects, for R/3, CRM and BW.

In fact, the overall concept stays the same for all SAP. The main difference is that you have different authorization objects of course, and also for Organizational management and stuff like IC WebClient you might want to read specific documentation on these topics if needed.

The main problem is that there is no specific guide with concrete examples of how to create authorizations. In most cases, a lot of trial and error is needed.

For now, I am not aware of any specific course to take to familiarize one's self with the authorization procedures.

Just know that the authorization objects are different. There are some documents on service.sap.com or help.sap.com specifically about CRM authorizations.

For example:

Authorization object
Authorization fields

CRM_ACT (authorization object CRM transaction – business transaction category activity)

ACTVT (activity)

CRM_CO_PU (authorization object CRM transaction – business transaction category purchase contract)

ACTVT

CRM_CO_SL (authorization object CRM transaction – business transaction category sales contract)

ACTVT

CRM_CO_SL (authorization object CRM transaction – business transaction category sales contract)

ACTVT

CRM_CO_SE (authorization object CRM transaction – business transaction category service contract)

ACTVT

CRM_CON_SE (authorization object CRM transaction – business transaction category service confirmation)

ACTVT

CRM_OPP (authorization object CRM transaction – business transaction category opportunity)

ACTVT

CRM_LEAD (authorization object CRM transaction – business transaction category lead)

ACTVT

CRM_CMP (authorization object CRM transaction – business transaction category complaint)

ACTVT

CRM_CO_SA (authorization object CRM transaction – business transaction category financing contract)

ACTVT

CRM_OPP_LP (authorization object CRM transaction – visibility in organization model)

CHECK_LEV (scope of processed objects)

PR_TYPE (transaction type)

ACTVT

CRM_OPP (authorization object CRM transaction – allowed organizational units)

SALES_ORG (sales organization)

SERVICE_OR (service organization)

DIS_CHANNE (distribution channel)

SALES_ORG (sales office)

SALES_GROU (sales group)

ACTVT

CRM_ORD_OP (authorization object CRM transaction – separate documents)

PARTN_FCT (partner function)

PARTN_FCTT (partner function category)

ACTVT

CRM_ORD_PR (authorization object CRM transaction – transaction type)

PR_TYPE (transaction type)

ACTVT

CRM_SAO (authorization object CRM transaction – business transaction category sales transaction)

ACTVT

CRM_SEO (authorization object CRM transaction – business transaction category service transaction)

ACTVT

☞ QUESTION 80

Organizational Structure Transport

I would like to know if it is possible to transport the Organizational Structure from Dev/Qa/Prod with a CRM 4.0.

✍ ANSWER

Yes it is possible. See Note 327908.

☞ QUESTION 81

ActiveX in MAS

Mobile Application Studio has already solved the problem to make a control ActiveX and to insert it in a Tile. My problem is I am not able to return the content of a property "Get from the control to Tile".

I can send and to receive data from the control ActiveX in the form that you describe but I need to rely on an event of BlueBox to send data to my ActiveX (without problem) or to add another control (a command button) and from this consent to the data of BlueBox. What I have not been able to do is to program an event in my control ActiveX (concretely the event click of a VSFLexGrid), and through a RaiseEvent in ActiveX to throw an event in MAS.

Does somebody know how to make it happen?

✍ ANSWER

There are two properties generated in the Class file of the Tile. One of them is for the BlueBox control itself and the other is for the control itself. Then in the TILE ONLOAD event you can access the Variable (This will be called CTRL< nameofblueboxcontrol>OBJ) and then access the variables of the ActiveX Control.

Have you written your own ActiveX Wrapper over FLEXGRID?

If yes, then your ActiveX control should raise an event by handling the event of FLEXGRID.

The process to handle an event is as follows:

BlueBox Control has an event. I do not remember the event name but it has only one event.

It has 2 parameters:

Signature would be something like this:
CTRL<nameofBluebox>_EVENTNAME (Info, Parameters);

This event will be raised in the Tile when an Event is raised in the inner
BlueBox control. You can then write custom code to handle the events

IF info.Value(0) = "ONCLICK" then
... Code
else if info.value(1) = "ONMOUSEOVER" then
... Code;

☞ QUESTION **82**

CALL List Dispatching Functionality in IC Webclient

Does anyone have experience or documentation on Call list dispatching for use in the Interaction Center Webclient?

We are trying to investigate this functionality to improve the performance of our outbound telesales scenario.

For a large call list (containing for example 5000 calls) we have long waiting times for displaying the call list en also for processing it. With the call list dispatching functionality we could somehow improve this according to SAP.

Where can I get more information on this subject?

✍ ANSWER

The way I did it was to modify ClmCallListDetailsGen.htm.

If you set ContCalls->CALL_LIST_RENDERING_MODE = '3', this by-passes the BOL and this speeds up the processing.

ContCalls->CALL_LIST_RENDERING_MODE = '3'.
lr_Calls = ContCalls->get_Calls_Table(iv_Large_View = Call_Iterator->Large_View iv_Selected_Id = lv_Call_Id).

☞ QUESTION **83**

Business Partner customer data

I enhanced business partner creation tab screen (/nBP) via Transaction code /nEEWB to add Sales Office field and it worked well. But when I tried to create BP via BAPI BAPI_BUPA_CREATE_FROM_DATA, I found no parameter that will enable the program to pass it on the sales office field.

What I am thinking now is to enhance the BAPI.

Is there any SAP Note regarding how to enhance the BAPI? For example: BAPI_BUPA_CREATE_FROM_DATA?

Is there any proper way besides enhancing BAPI_BUPA_CREATE_FROM_DATA?

✍ **ANSWER**

Use function 'BUPA_CENTRAL_CI_CHANGE' after you

☞ QUESTION 84

CICO Transaction - Applied area or Navigation area Tab can't be displayed

There is a problem in Transaction CICO in our Production System.

The Problem is:

1. When I execute transaction CICO, it displays Interaction Center WinClient;

2. When I enter data in Business Partner under Field Partner, it displays the data.

3. However, when I choose Application Area or Navigation Area, the page cannot be displayed in View (80% Overview Screen).

The Development and Quality system works fine.

What could be the problem and how could this be resolved?

✍ ANSWER

There are some things you need to do:

First of all, I will advise you to check all transport requests (did you get return code 0?);

Secondly, I would double check your customizing settings specifically those related to navigation area (compare CRQ with your CRP system).

*You also might want to check on OSS notes:

*CRM-CIC-INB 0000859781 0001 0.700 CIC IBASE navigation area search by object id is n;

*CRM-CIC-FRW 0000582125 0011 0.510 How to get Application Area as Full Screen?

*CRM-CIC-INB 0000849344 0001 0.360 Performance Problems in IBASE Search in CIC0;

*CRM-CIC-PRO-INF 0000806240 0001 0.430 search result of product list is not sorted in CIC;

*CRM-CIC-FRW 0000765820 0002 0.460 Layout-switch brings error message "SET SCREEN not;

*CRM-CIC-BTRANSACTION 0000742144 0001 0.440 Partner pushbutton in Transaction CIC0 has no effect;

*CRM-CIC-HIS-IHI 0000695837 0001 0.390 no secondary sorting of trans. in Tab 'Interaction;

Without looking at the systems, it is impossible to give a specific answer to your question for a diagnosis.

If you really want to know the source of the problem, check further all UserParameters if they are the same.

There exist specific user parameters for IC:

CRM_ICWC_SHORTCUTS
CRM_ICWC_STATIC

However, I don't think they will matter in this case.

If you are using IC WebClient, also check your Java runtime environment, because this needs to be of a certain version.

Another thing you could check is Authorizations (do a trace via ST01 or su53).

After finding out what is wrong, the resolution of the problem will be easier.

☞ QUESTION **85**

Find BSP View name on Web IC

Does anyone know an easy way of finding out the name of a view on the web IC?

For example, if I was looking at the inbox items, is there a way to tell that the view I am looking at is auiItems.htm?

✍ ANSWER

You can create a new Parameter ID CRM_ICWC_TEST on your user. It should have a value of 0XX3456789.

☞ QUESTION 86

Fact Sheet not displaying Quick Info or Last 20 activities

When the fact sheet is displayed in CRM middleware under BP, the Contacts and Classification details are displayed but an error occurs when Quick Info or Last 20 Activities is selected. The Business Partner Cockpit behaves in the same way.

How can I resolve this issue?

✍ ANSWER

For most problems there is already a solution available via OSS notes.

Look for transaction code: OSS1. Otherwise use service.sap. com to search for other OSS notes.

Another possibility is OSS 490871. This is a COMPOSITE note on the Business partner Cockpit and Fact sheet Issues. You also get per info block a list of possible OSS notes.

☞ QUESTION 87

The locator's search range

The locator's default search range is limited in 100.

How do break pass this limit?

✍ ANSWER

The locator is just a series of search helps.

You could try modifying the search helps to bring back more than 100 records. However, the easiest way is simply to modify your search criteria so that the records you want are returned.

☞ **QUESTION 88**

COM_PARTNER_BADI

I have implemented the BADI. The required code is written in Method DETERMINATION_ADD_IN_1. We have also defined an Access Sequence with Source as Business Add_in 1.

What else should be done in Access Sequences so that the BADI gets triggered?

The BADI is for Partner Determination based on the Rule. This rule resolution is done based on Product ID?

✍ **ANSWER**

For the same requirement, I have used a different BADI COM_PARTNER_BADI got already triggered way before you enter product.

Implement the following definition and you should be able to determine a partner based product entered by the user:

CRM_PRODUCT_I_BADI.

☞ QUESTION **89**

Print Opportunity

In the screen of Opportunities in the PCUI the button for 'Print' is not selectable.

Why aren't we able to print an opportunity?

✍ ANSWER

The Output is issued in CRM transaction through Actions. You need an action profile with an Action to generate output assigned to the document type.

☞ QUESTION 90

IPC User exit

We have a scenario wherein we would like to give a discount for certain materials.

So we thought of using a Zcondition type to which a routine would be attached, this condition type would then be attached to the pricing schema. All the pricing calculations are done in the IPC.

I also need to attach a pricing routine to the schema in SRM and then write the Java user exit in IPC. We are currently using SRM release 3.0.

How should I proceed to achieve this?

✍ ANSWER

You need to modify the PricingUserExits.java file on the IPC server.

Look for the line: public int[] getConditionValueFormulaNumbers(){;

Delete the line underneath: return new int[] { };

Replace with: return new int[] { 901 }; where 901 is your routine number.

Add your new routine to the CrmPricingUserExits file within the following statement: switch (valueFormNo) {your routine goes here};

You also need to update the "customerexits.properties" file to include your new routine.

☞ QUESTION 91

Change an order in R/3 replicated from CRM

Can I change an order in R/3 replicated from CRM?

✍ ANSWER

If the order is created in CRM and replicated to R/3 you can make changes to that order like change quantity or products, etc. But the document created in R/3 & replicated to CRM cannot have any changes.

In the R/3 adapter, you can define your "data exchange scenario" this setting directly effects where documents can or should be changed and which system has "ownership" of a document.

The options you have for data exchange scenario depend on which version of R/3 and CRM you are running.

The data exchange scenario is defined in CRMPAROLTP table in R/3.

There are quite a few OSS notes that describe your options. Do a search for this table and the data exchange scenario and you should find them.

See note 642944 and related ones.

☞ QUESTION 92

Error PPR item in sales contract

I'm trying to do a sales contract without reference to other document. When I input a product, the system gives me an error related to PPR. However, the same document copy with reference doesn't return any error. I don't have any customizing related to PPR.

How can I resolve this issue?

✍ ANSWER

Find SAP Notes 839963 and 850919 and go through them. This will solve your problem.

☞ QUESTION **93**

Problems related with BADI's

I need help in getting the answer to the following questions:

1. How do we know where one BADI, say CRM_MKTPL (name of BADI) is being used. How do I know which application is to be run for catching the code written in the method of that particular BADI?

2. In SE18, when we open any BADI, there is one option of checking the check box "multiple uses". What is the function of that option?

3. One BADI can have multiple implementations. If a BADI has been called, how do we know which implementation has to be used?

✍ **ANSWER**

Try and check transaction SE84.

Open folder Enhancements > Business Add-Inn> Definitions: find the definition and open;

Now menu path Implementation > Display;

You will have a list of all implementations for the BADI.

☞ QUESTION 94

BADI for change activity

What is the BADI for activity change?

1. Description.
2. Goal.

We want to change the fields of the activity onsave.

✍ ANSWER

The BADI you need to implement is BADI CRM Order Save.
Use transaction se18.

You need to use the method called PREPARE.

Here are some code I used to change the description
Data : it_orderadm_h TYPE crmt_orderadm_h_comt,
is_orderadm_h TYPE crmt_orderadm_h_com,
ls_input_field TYPE crmt_input_field,
lt_input_field TYPE crmt_input_field_tab.

is_orderadm_h-description = lv_description.
is_orderadm_h-guid = iv_guid.
INSERT is_orderadm_h INTO TABLE it_orderadm_h.

ls_input_field-ref_guid = iv_guid.
ls_input_field-objectname = gc_object_name-orderadm_h.
ls_input_names-fieldname = 'DESCRIPTION'.
INSERT ls_input_names INTO TABLE ls_input_field-field_
names.
INSERT ls_input_field INTO TABLE lt_input_field.

```
CALL FUNCTION 'CRM_ORDER_MAINTAIN'
CHANGING
ct_orderadm_h = it_orderadm_h
ct_input_fields = lt_input_field
EXCEPTIONS
error_occurred = 1
document_locked = 2
no_change_allowed = 3
no_authority = 4
OTHERS = 5.
```

The program crm_order_read is a useful program to see what fields structures are used for business transactions:

crm_order_read - read an activity

Some additional information:

1. Implement the badi order_save.
2. You make your code changes in the PREPARE method.
3. Modify the following code. This code changes the description of an activity record.

```
INCLUDE crm_object_names_con.
INCLUDE crm_object_kinds_con.

Data : it_orderadm_h TYPE crmt_orderadm_h_comt,
is_orderadm_h TYPE crmt_orderadm_h_com,
ls_input_field TYPE crmt_input_field,
lt_input_field TYPE crmt_input_field_tab.

* This is the only line of code you have to change
is_orderadm_h-description = 'NEW DESCRIPTION'
is_orderadm_h-guid = iv_guid. "Passed in by the BADI
```

INSERT is_orderadm_h INTO TABLE it_orderadm_h.

* NO FURTHER CODE CHANGES - CUT AND PASTE

ls_input_field-ref_guid = iv_guid.
ls_input_field-objectname = gc_object_name-orderadm_h.
ls_input_names-fieldname = 'DESCRIPTION'.
INSERT ls_input_names INTO TABLE ls_input_field-field_names.
INSERT ls_input_field INTO TABLE lt_input_field.

CALL FUNCTION 'CRM_ORDER_MAINTAIN'
CHANGING
ct_orderadm_h = it_orderadm_h
ct_input_fields = lt_input_field
EXCEPTIONS
error_occurred = 1
document_locked = 2
no_change_allowed = 3
no_authority = 4
OTHERS = 5.

General steps:

1. Put the above code into the BADI.
2. Activate the BADI implementation in se19.
3. Put a break point in the BADI code.
4. Create an Activity.
5. Save the activity.
6. The above code will be executed.

☞ QUESTION 95

b2b logon error

We have finished creating webshop using http://host:port/shopadmin/shopadmin/init.do?scenario.xcm = your scenario.

Now while trying to login at http://host:port/b2b/b2b/init.do , it says the catalog is not valid for this webshop. We followed the CRM building blocks and went step by step.

I cannot locate where the problem is. How do I resolve this?

✍ ANSWER

Check XCM configuration for webcatalog component.

Make sure that it is pointing to webserver and not to webserver/catalog.

Parameter for image server: http://<your web server>.

Don't give /catalog.

☞ **QUESTION 96**

Product catalog not visible in b2b webshop

Product catalog not visible in b2b webshop: Http://hots:port/b2b/b2b/init.do.

After logging in I am not able to see the product catalog. I checked the log of index server. It is properly replicated.

I have configured b2b shop using XCM and when I tried to login it asks to select a shop. Once I select a shop, it asks for select a 'sold to party' and once it is selected I enter into webshop. There I am not able to see any products but the info created a new order or it creates a new order template. All this stuff is visible but when I click on the product catalog it says 'no products available'. I have created product catalog in CRM and successfully replicated them to TREX. I can see the indexes in TREX.

I have activated catalog at all levels and have maintained only one view and assigned a contact person to it who has 'sold to party' belonging to the same sales area of catalog variant and materials.

How can I resolve this issue?

✍ **ANSWER**

It is an XCM configuration problem. When you mention image server under the components configuration in XCM, make sure that you are only giving the location of the webserver.

Example: your catalog is on webserver crmtst1.

You have to give image server as http://crmtst1.

Not http://crmtst1/catalog.

☞ QUESTION 97

To add custom fields to Opportunity Screen

How do I add custom fields to Opportunity Screen?

Are there any user exits or BADI's for this?

Or do I need to use screen painter and directly modify from that?

I am also trying to add new custom tab and z-fields in it.

✍ ANSWER

Use EEWB (easy enhancement workbench) first.

You can add new fields or table (in this case, key field should be defined) using this tool the easy way.

During work with EEWB, you may choose from:

1. Standard Header Table
2. Standard Item Table
3. Predefined Customer Table

☞ **QUESTION 98**

BDC for SAP-CRM using transaction 'CRMD_BUS2000115'

I am a technical person who wanted to run BDC for transaction 'CRMD_BUS2000115'. However, in the recording itself I am not able to capture the details i.e. where the product & quantity entries should go to. These are not getting captured in BDC.

I do not want to enter manual entries, since I have 300 entries. I am trying to use BDC for uploading.

Is it possible?

✍ **ANSWER**

Try the BAPI or Function Modules (XIF).

If you are trying to create activities you can try BAPI_ACTIVITYCRM_CREATEMULTI.

☞ QUESTION 99

Customizing the Business Partner (BP) transaction view

I am looking for a way in which I can customize the view. I would like to check which fields can be added in transaction BP (Master Data-> Business Partner->Maintain Business Partners.

How can this be done?

✍ ANSWER

Try transaction BUPT.

You can also try visual configuration tool "VCT" under IMG.

VCT is easier to use than BDT (BUPT).

☞ QUESTION 100

Regarding XIF Interface and Sale Transaction in CRM

I am doing the ALE setup for CRM using XIF adapter of the CRM system.

I completed the ALE configuration in the CRM system using XIF interface to communicate with other system (In our case it is SAP SRM system).

When I create a sales transaction using transaction code CRMD_ORDER, the system allows me to save/create a business transaction even though I can see some basic error attached to it (since we are in process of CRM implementation and some master data like partner is not yet uploaded to the system). At the same time I can see the BDOC number in SMW01.

What I don't see is any relevant OUTBOUND IDOC against the BDOC, even if I have configured it for the external system and I was expecting Outbound IDOC with error status.

Am I wrong in assuming that this should be automated?

I am using WE02 and WE05 to see my OUTBOUND IDOC and I have not found anything there.

Am I missing some step in configuration which is required for converting BDOC to IDOC?

The steps which I followed to configure the system are as

follows:

1. Create a suitable RFC destination in the SAP IMG Define Target Systems for RFC Calls.

2. Create a logical system.

3. Create a receiver port (transactional RFC) in SAP IMG Define Port, indicating the RFC destination you created earlier.

4. Create a partner profile, for example, partner type LS.

5. Enter all outbound parameters for the logical system.

6. Create a site (transaction SMOEAC). To do this, select Object Type Sites and Create Object. Assign your site a suitable name and select Site Type External Interface for IDOC's. Assign the partner profile created previously as a Site Attribute.

7. Use object type Subscriptions to maintain a subscription for publication of the object with the predefined site.

8. Create an entry for the new site using XIF customizing transaction CRMXIF_C1 via F4 help (BDOC Type = <objname>, IF Type = 'CRMXIF_*_SAVE_M', Set relevant flag for complete Data and Return). The flag for complete data is only relevant for the objects "order", "business partner", and "business partner relationship". It flags whether only delta changes or the object instance should be transferred completely. The object "business document" is always sent completely, regardless of flag status.

✍ ANSWER

There is a possibility that because of incomplete business data, XIF interface is not creating the corresponding IDOC.

I know for a fact that the R/3 interface is not called if there are errors. I'm not sure about IDOC interface, but if the behavior for all sites in SMOEAC isn't coherent; the interface will not be called.

Try sending the order with report CRMXIF_ORDER_TEST. It uses functions CRMXIF_ORDER_MAPSEND & CRMXIF_ORDER_EXTRACT to extract the information and send it to the XIF site (be it an IDOC or an XML). If necessary, you can debug by setting a break-point on the functions and see if the extract is performed.

Yes, "post it immediately" is correct (for tests at least).

Your problem could be related to the error you're getting in CRM. As I said earlier, at least for the R/3 interface, the errors would be the reason for the absence of communication.

In SMW01, if you select the BDOC corresponding to order, and press the "errors" button you should get two options: 'List errors and list receivers'. In the list receivers, make sure your XIF site is there, and in the error list, check for a line that says something like "No upload into <site>".

INDEX

Attention SAP Experts

Have you ever considered writing a book in your area of SAP? Equity Press is the leading provider of knowledge products in SAP applications consulting, development, and support. If you have a manuscript or an idea of a manuscript, we'd love to help you get it published!

Please send your manuscript or manuscript ideas to jim@sapcookbook.com – we'll help you turn your dream into a reality.

Or mail your inquiries to:

Equity Press Manuscripts
BOX 706
Riverside, California
92502

Tel (951)788-0810
Fax (951)788-0812

50% Off your next
SAPCOOKBOOK order

If you plan of placing an order for 10 or more books from www.sapcookbook.com you qualify for volume discounts. Please send an email to books@sapcookbook.com or phone 951-788-0810 to place your order.

You can also fax your orders to 951-788-0812 .

Interview books are great for cross-training

In the new global economy, the more you know the better. The sharpest consultants are doing everything they can to pick up more than one functional area of SAP. Each of the following Certification Review / Interview Question books provides an excellent starting point for your module learning and investigation. These books get you started like no other book can – by providing you the information that you really need to know, and fast.

SAPCOOKBOOK Interview Questions, Answers, and Explanations

ABAP	-	SAP ABAP Certification Review: SAP ABAP Interview Questions, Answers, and Explanations
SD	-	SAP SD Interview Questions, Answers, and Explanations
Security	-	SAP Security: SAP Security Essentials
HR	-	mySAP HR Interview Questions, Answers, and Explanations: SAP HR Certification Review
BW	-	SAP BW Ultimate Interview Questions, Answers, and Explanations: SAW BW Certification Review
	-	SAP SRM Interview Questions Answers and Explanations
Basis	-	SAP Basis Certification Questions: Basis Interview Questions, Answers, and Explanations
MM	-	SAP MM Certification and Interview Questions: SAP MM Interview Questions, Answers, and Explanations

SAP BW Ultimate Interview Questions, Answers, and Explanations

Key Topics Include:

- The most important BW settings to know
- BW tables and transaction code quick references
- Certification Examination Questions
- Extraction, Modeling and Configuration
- Transformations and Administration
- Performance Tuning, Tips & Tricks, and FAQ
- Everything a BW resource needs to know before an interview

mySAP HR Interview Questions, Answers, and Explanations

Key topics include:

- The most important HR settings to know
- mySAP HR Administration tables and transaction code quick references
- SAP HR Certification Examination Questions
- Org plan, Compensation, Year End, Wages, and Taxes
- User Management, Transport System, Patches, and Upgrades
- Benefits, Holidays, Payroll, and Infotypes
- Everything an HR resource needs to know before an interview

SAP SRM Interview Questions, Answers, and Explanations

Key Topics Include:

- The most important SRM Configuration to know
- Common EBP Implementation Scenarios
- Purchasing Document Approval Processes
- Supplier Self Registration and Self Service (SUS)
- Live Auctions and Bidding Engine, RFX Processes (LAC)
- Details for Business Intelligence and Spend Analysis
- EBP Technical and Troubleshooting Information

SAP MM Interview Questions, Answers, and Explanations

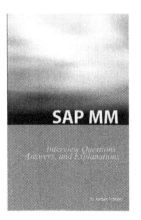

- The most important MM Configuration to know
- Common MM Implementation Scenarios
- MM Certification Exam Questions
- Consumption Based Planning
- Warehouse Management
- Material Master Creation and Planning
- Purchasing Document Inforecords

SAP SD Interview Questions, Answers, and Explanations

- The most important SD settings to know
- SAP SD administration tables and transaction code quick references
- SAP SD Certification Examination Questions
- Sales Organization and Document Flow Introduction
- Partner Procedures, Backorder Processing, Sales BOM
- Backorder Processing, Third Party Ordering, Rebates and Refunds
- Everything an SD resource needs to know before an interview

SAP Basis Interview Questions, Answers, and Explanations

- The most important Basis settings to know
- Basis Administration tables and transaction code quick references
- Certification Examination Questions
- Oracle database, UNIX, and MS Windows Technical Information
- User Management, Transport System, Patches, and Upgrades
- Backup and Restore, Archiving, Disaster Recover, and Security
- Everything a Basis resource needs to know before an interview

SAP Security Essentials

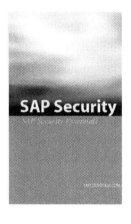

- Finding Audit Critical Combinations
- Authentication, Transaction Logging, and Passwords
- Roles, Profiles, and User Management
- ITAR, DCAA, DCMA, and Audit Requirements
- The most important security settings to know
- Security Tuning, Tips & Tricks, and FAQ
- Transaction code list and table name references

SAP Workflow Interview Questions, Answers, and Explanations

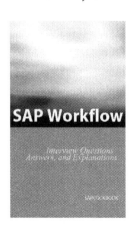

- Database Updates and Changing the Standard
- List Processing, Internal Tables, and ALV Grid Control
- Dialog Programming, ABAP Objects
- Data Transfer, Basis Administration
- ABAP Development reference updated for 2006!
- Everything an ABAP resource needs to know before an interview